junie b. jones®

Is a Party Animal

by BARBARA PARK

illustrated by

Denise Brunkus

Long tail Books

Junie B. Jones Is a Party Animal

This bilingual edition was published by Longtail Books in 2022 by arrangement with Barbara Park c/o Writers House LLC through KCC(Korea Copyright Center Inc.), Seoul.

ISBN 979-11-91343-17-5 14740

Longtail, Inc.

Contents

1. The Richiest Nanna 5
2. Excellent Work of Us 14
3. The Rules 24
4. Packing My Bags 31
5. Going to the Ball 42
6. Bouncing 59
7. Peeping 80
8. Morning 84

1
The Richiest[1] Nanna

My name is Junie B. Jones. The B **stand**s **for** Beatrice. **Except** I don't like Beatrice. I just like B and **that's all**.

I am almost six years old.

Almost six is when you **ride** the bus to afternoon **kindergarten**.

---

1 **richiest** 형용사 'rich'의 최상급을 잘못 만든 것으로, 올바른 표현은 'richest'이다.

My bestest[2] friend named Grace rides the bus with me.

Every day she sits right **exact**ly next to me. 'Cause I save her a seat, that's why.

Saving a seat is when you **zoom** on the bus. And you hurry up and sit down. And then you quick put your feet on the seat next to you.

After that, you keep on **scream**ing the word "SAVED! SAVED! SAVED!" And no one even sits next to you. 'Cause who wants to sit next to a screamer? That's what I would like to know.

Me and that Grace have another bestest friend at school. Her name is Lucille.

---

2 **bestest** 단어 'best(최고의)'를 강조한 비격식적인 표현. '최고로 좋은'이라는 뜻을 나타내며 어린아이가 주로 사용한다.

Lucille does not ride the bus with us. Her richie[3] nanna drives her to school in a big gold car. It is called a Cattle Act,[4] I think.

And guess what?

Today that big gold Cattle Act was driving right next to the school bus!

I **bang**ed on my window very excited.

"LUCILLE! HEY, LUCILLE! IT'S ME! IT'S JUNIE B. JONES! I AM RIGHT NEXT TO YOU ON THE SCHOOL BUS! SEE ME? SEE ME, LUCILLE? I AM BANGING ON MY WINDOW VERY EXCITED!"

---

3 **richie** '부유한'이라는 뜻의 'rich'를 주니 B.가 'richie'라고 장난스럽게 말한 표현. 이 책에 나오는 'all rightie(all right)', 'okie doke(okey doke)' 등이 이와 같은 경우이다.

4 **Cattle Act** 주니 B.가 미국의 고급 승용차 'Cadillac(캐딜락)'을 잘못 알아듣고 말한 것이다.

Lucille did not see me.

"YEAH, ONLY HERE'S THE PROBLEM! YOUR NANNA JUST **SPEED**ED UP HER CAR. AND NOW YOU ARE ZOOMING WAY AHEAD OF THE BUS. AND SO HOW COME I AM STILL SHOUTING AT YOU? THAT'S WHAT I WOULD LIKE TO KNOW."

I sat down and **smooth**ed my skirt.

"Lucille's nanna has a lead foot,[5] **apparent**ly," I said to that Grace.

"Lucille's nanna is rich," she said back.

"Lucille's nanna is very, *very* rich," I said. "She owns a big, **giant** house with a **million** rooms in it. And she lets Lucille's

---

5 **lead foot** '스피드광', '폭주족'이라는 뜻으로 지나치게 빠르게 운전하는 사람을 비유적으로 나타내는 표현.

whole **entire** family live there. 'Cause it is way too big for just one nanna."

"Wow," said that Grace.

"I know it is wow, Grace," I said. "My nanna just owns a **plain**, old, **regular** house, and **that's it**."

That Grace did a sad **sigh**.

"My nanna just owns a condo[6] in Florida," she said.

Then me and that Grace looked at each other very **glum**.

"Our nannas are **losers**," I said.

After that, we didn't talk the rest of the trip.

Only guess what?

---

6 **condo** 콘도. 미국의 분양 아파트로 주로 리조트에 건설되어 있으며, 숙박 시설 외에도 레저 시설을 갖추고 있다.

When we got to school, we saw the nanna's big gold car! It was parked right in the **parking lot**!

Me and that Grace runned[7] there **speedy** fast.

"Lucille! Lucille! It's me! It's Junie B. Jones! Plus also it's that Grace! We are running to see your richie nanna!"

We opened the door and **stick**ed our heads inside.

"Hi, Nanna!" I said.

"Hello, Nanna!" said that Grace.

The nanna looked surprised at us.

"Yeah, only you don't even have to be

---

7 **runned** (ran) 영어권 국가의 아이들이 동사의 과거형을 말할 때 모든 단어의 끝에 '-ed'를 붙이는 실수를 종종 한다. 이 책에 나오는 'swinged(swung)', 'springed(sprang)' 등이 이와 같은 경우이다.

afraid of us," I said. "'Cause we know your grandgirl very good. Plus we won't even **harm** you."

Me and that Grace got in the back.

I **rub**bed my hand on the seat.

"Oooo! I love this rich **velvety**[8] **interior**," I told her.

I put my **cheek** on it.

"These seats are ooo-la-la,[9] Nanna," I said.

Lucille looked **grouchy** at me. "Don't call her *nanna!* She's *my* nanna! Not *your* nanna!"

"Lucille!" said the nanna very shocked.

---

8 **velvet** 벨벳. 짧고 부드러운 솜털이 광택을 내는 고급 원단.

9 **ooo-la-la** '멋지다', '놀랍다'라는 뜻으로 놀람이나 감탄 등을 나타내는 표현.

"What's gotten into you? Your little friends are **darling**."

"Yes, Lucille," I said. "I am darling. Plus that Grace is darling. And so, **back off**. Right, Nanna?"

The nanna did a loud **hoot** of laughing.

"Hey! You are the **friendliest** nanna I ever saw!" I said. "And so maybe me and

Grace can come see your richie house sometime."

Lucille's nanna did another loud hoot.

Then me and that Grace did loud hoots, too. And all of us kept on laughing and laughing.

Only not Lucille.

2
Excellent Work of Us

Lucille sits at my same table in Room Nine.

She kept on being mad at me. Only I don't even know why.

"That is a lovely sweater you are wearing today, Lucille," I said very **pleasant**.

She **scoot**ed her chair away from me.

I scooted next to her.

"Oooo. Is that sequins[1] I see on the **collar**? 'Cause sequins are my favorite little, **shiny**, **roundish beady** things," I told her.

I touched one of the sequins.

Lucille pushed my hand away.

I **tickle**d her under the **chin** very **friendly**.

"Coochie-coochie-coo,[2]" I said real fun.

Lucille turned her back to me.

I **swing**ed her ponytail.[3]

"Swingy,[4] swingy, swingy," I sang.

---

1 **sequin** 스팽글. 금속, 플라스틱 등으로 만들어진 반짝거리는 얇은 장식 조각. 주로 무대 의상이나 핸드백, 구두 등에 붙인다.

2 **coochie-coochie-coo** 아기들을 귀여워하며 달랠 때 내는 소리인 'coochy coo'를 주니 B.가 장난스럽게 말한 표현.

3 **ponytail** 포니테일. 긴 머리를 뒷머리 위쪽에서 리본 등으로 묶고 머리 끝을 망아지 꼬리처럼 늘어뜨린 머리 형태의 하나.

Just then, Lucille **spring**ed out of her chair.

"STOP TOUCHING ME!" she **holler**ed right in my face.

My teacher hurried to my table **speedy** fast.

Her name is Mrs.

She has another name, too. But I just like Mrs. and **that's all**.

I smiled at her very cute.

"Hello. How are you today? Me and Lucille are not even fighting. We are just having a **loudish conservation**."

Mrs. looked funny at me.

---

4 **swingy** 주니 B.가 만들어 낸 말로 단어 'swing(흔들다)'의 뒤에 '-y'를 붙여 '흔들리는'이라는 의미의 형용사로 사용하였다. 이 책에 나오는 'scrunchy', 'twisty' 등도 이와 같은 경우이다.

"I think you mean ***conversation,*** Junie B.," she said. "*Conservation* is when people save something."

I **tap**ped on my chin very thinking.

Then **all of a sudden**, I jumped up real excited.

"Yeah, only I *do,* Mrs.! I *do* save something!" I said. "I save that Grace a seat on the bus!"

I shouted across the room. "GRACE! HEY, GRACE! TELL MRS. HOW I SAVE YOU A SEAT ON THE BUS! 'CAUSE SHE THINKS I DON'T KNOW MY WORDS, **APPARENT**LY!"

That Grace shouted back. "SHE DOES, TEACHER! JUNIE B. SAVES ME A SEAT ON THE BUS EVERY SINGLE DAY!"

I smiled very **proud**. "See, Mrs.? I told

you! I told you I save something!"

Mrs. **stare**d at me a real long time.

Then she closed her eyes.

And she said she needs a **vacation**.

Pretty soon, the bell rang for **recess**.

Lucille didn't even wait for me and Grace. She runned right out the door without us.

That is how come we had to **chase** that girl down and **surround** her.

I made my voice very **growly**.

"I am at the end of my string[5] with you, madam![6]" I said. "How come you keep

---

5 **at the end of one's string** '인내심이 한계에 달한'이라는 뜻의 숙어.

6 **madam** '계집애'라는 뜻으로 건방진 여자아이를 얕잡아 부를 때 사용하는 비격식적인 호칭.

being mad at us? 'Cause me and Grace didn't even do anything to you!"

Lucille **stamp**ed her foot.

"Yes, you did! You **ruin**ed everything! I was **beg**ging my **nanna** for a little white poodle![7] And she was almost going to say yes! And then you guys got in my **backseat**! And now everything is ruined!"

I did a **huffy** breath at her.

"Yeah, only that is not even our **fault**, Lucille! 'Cause we didn't know you were begging! We just wanted to see your richie nanna, and that's all!"

"I don't care!" said Lucille. "You should have stayed away! You guys have your *own*

---

7 **poodle** 푸들. 개의 한 품종으로 양털 모양의 긴 털이 특징이다. 영리하고 사람을 잘 따라 애완용으로 많이 기른다.

nannas!"

Just then, me and that Grace got very **glum** again.

"I *know* we have nannas, Lucille," I said. "But they are not *richie* nannas like yours."

That Grace **hang**ed **her head**.

"Our nannas are just ***regular*** nannas," she said.

"They are **dud**s," I said real soft.

After that, Lucille acted nicer to us.

"Sorry," she said. "Sorry about your regular nannas. I was just **upset** about not getting my poodle, that's all. Usually my nanna gives me whatever I want."

Just then, I smiled real big. 'Cause a great idea **pop**ped in my head, that's why! It came right out of thin hair![8]

"Lucille! Hey, Lucille! Maybe me and Grace can come to your nanna's house! And we can help you beg for a poodle!"

I danced all around.

"And here is *another* great idea! Maybe we can even spend the night, possibly! 'Cause me and Grace never even saw a richie house before! Plus that way we can beg for your poodle the whole **entire** evening!"

All of a sudden, that Grace started dancing all around, too. "When can we come? When can we come?" she asked.

I **clap**ped my hands very **thrill**ed.

"I am **available** on Saturday, I believe!" I

---

8 **out of thin hair** 숙어 'out of thin air(갑자기, 난데없이)'의 'air'를 주니 B.가 'hair'로 잘못 알아듣고 말한 표현.

said.

"Me, too! I am available on Saturday, too!" said that Grace.

Lucille thought and thought.

"Hmm. I don't know about Saturday," she said. "My mommy and daddy and brother are going away for the weekend. So it's just going to be my nanna and me."

I jumped up and down.

"**Hurray**!" I said. "That will **work out** even better! 'Cause now we can beg your nanna with **positive**ly no **interruption**s!"

Just then, Lucille started to smile.

"Hey, yeah! Why didn't *I* think of that?" she said.

I pointed at myself.

"'Cause I'm the brains of this **outfit**,

that's why!" I said real happy.

After that, all of us **skip**ped around and around.

Plus me and that Grace did a **high five**.

'CAUSE WE WERE ON OUR WAY TO THE NANNA'S, OF COURSE!!!

3
The Rules

Guess what!!?! Guess what!!?!

On Friday, Lucille's nanna called my mother!

And she invited me to spend the night with Lucille on Saturday!

And Mother didn't even say no!

My feet **zoom**ed all around the house when I heard that!

"I'M SPENDIN' THE NIGHT! I'M

SPENDIN' THE NIGHT! I'M SPENDIN' THE NIGHT!" I shouted.

I zoomed into my baby brother Ollie's room.

"HEY, OLLIE! I'M SPENDIN' THE NIGHT! I'M SPENDIN' THE NIGHT! I'M SPENDIN' THE—"

Just then, Mother runned in the door and she **swish**ed me right out of there.

It was not **pleasant**.

I **brush**ed myself off.

"Yeah, only you shouldn't actually swish people," I said kind of quiet.

Mother raised her voice at me.

"How many times, Junie B.? How many times have I told you to stay out of Ollie's room while he's sleeping? Huh? How many?"

I thinked for a minute.

"A **million bazillion**," I said. "But that is just a **ballpark figure**."

Mother **glare**d at me very mad.

I **rock**ed **back and forth** on my feet.

"A ballpark figure is when you don't know the actual figure. And so you **make up** a figure. 'Cause that will **get** people **off your back**," I explained. "My boyfriend named Ricardo told me that. His father sells **insurance**, I believe."

Mother **tap**ped her angry foot.

"We are *not* talking about Ricardo's father, Junie B. We are talking about going into Ollie's room while he's sleeping. And **besides**, I haven't said that you could spend the night at Lucille's. I want to **talk** it

over with your father first."

I **hug**ged her leg.

"Please, Mother? Please? Please? I'll be good. I promise, I promise, I—"

Just then, the front door opened.

It was my Daddy!

He was home from work!

I runned to him like a speedy rocket.

Then I hugged his leg, too. And he couldn't even shake me off.

"I'll be good, Daddy! I promise! I promise! I promise!"

All of a sudden, Mother swished me away again. She put me down in the living room.

Then she and Daddy did **whisper**ing in the **hall**.

And guess what?

They said I could go to Lucille's!!!

"YIPPEE![1] YIPPEE! YIPPEE!" I shouted.

After that, I started to zoom some more. But Daddy quick **grab**bed me by my belt.

"Yeah, only here's the problem. I'm not actually zooming," I told him.

"No . . . *here's* the problem," said Daddy. "Before you spend the night with Lucille, you have to agree to the rules."

I raised up my **eyebrow**s.

"Rules?" I asked. "There's rules **involve**d?"

"*Lots* of rules," said Daddy.

Then he and Mother **bend**ed down

---

1 **yippee** '야호', '만세'라는 뜻으로 기쁨을 표현하는 감탄사.

next to me. And they told me the rules of spending the night.

They are: *No running, no jumping, no shouting, no* ***squeal****ing, no* ***holler****ing, no* ***snoop****ing, no* ***spy****ing, no* ***arguing****, no fighting, no* ***cheat****ing at games, no talking back to the nanna, no breaking other people's toys, no* ***grump****ing, no crying, no* ***fib****bing, no* ***tickling*** *people when they say no, no staying up late, and* ***absolute****ly no* ***head-butt****ing.*

After I heard the rules, I did a **sigh**.

"Yeah, only that doesn't actually leave me much to work with," I said.

Mother **ruffle**d my hair.

"Sorry, kiddo.[2] But that's the **deal**," she

---

2 **kiddo** '애', '자네', '젊은이'라는 뜻으로 자신보다 나이가 어린 상대방을 호의적인 태도로 부를 때 사용하는 비격식적인 호칭.

said. "Take it or leave it.[3]"

"Take it!" I shouted out. "I'll take the deal!"

Then I kissed Mother and Daddy on their **cheek**s.

And I hugged them very tight.

And they couldn't shake me off again.

---

3 **take it or leave it** '싫으면 그만두다', '승낙 여부는 당신 마음대로다'라는 뜻의 숙어.

4
Packing My Bags

The next morning was Saturday.

I jumped out of bed and runned to the kitchen.

Then I got a big, **giant** plastic bag. And I runned back to my room to pack for Lucille's.

First, I packed my favorite **pillow**. Then I packed my **pajamas** and my bath**robe** and my **slipper**s that look like bunnies. Also, I packed my **blanket** and my **sheet**s and a small, **attractive** throw **rug**.

Finally, I packed my **stuff**ed elephant named Philip Johnny Bob.

He looked up at me from inside the bag. *Yeah, only here's the problem,* he said. *You'**re** not actually **supposed to** put me in a plastic bag. 'Cause I could **suffercate**[1] in this thing.*

My eyes got big and wide.

"Oh no!" I said real **upset**. "I forgot about that!"

That's how come I quick got my scissors and cut air holes for that guy.

Philip Johnny Bob **sniff**ed the air. *Better,*

---

1 **suffercate** 주니 B.가 '질식사하다'라는 뜻의 'suffocate'를 잘못 말한 것이다.

he said.

I **pet**ted his **trunk**. Then I went into the **family room**. And I watched **cartoon**s till Mother got up.

Pretty soon, I heard her slippers in the **hall**.

"MOTHER! MOTHER! I'M ALL READY!" I said. "I'M ALL READY TO GO TO LUCILLE'S!"

I pulled Mother into my room and showed her my plastic bag.

Mother shook her head. "Waaaay too much stuff," she said.

Then she got a **teeny suitcase** from the **shelf**. And she packed my pajamas and my slippers and my robe and my **toothbrush**.

After that, she got a **sleeping bag** from

her **closet**. And she put my pillow on top of it.

"There. That's all you'll need. You**'re all set**," she said.

I **spring**ed into the air.

"ALL SET!" I hollered real **joyful**. "JUNIE B. JONES IS ALL SET FOR LUCILLE'S!"

After that, I quick **grab**bed Philip Johnny Bob. And I **drag**ged my stuff to the front door.

"ALL RIGHTIE! LET'S BE ON OUR WAY!" I shouted very excited.

Mother was in baby Ollie's room. She didn't come.

"OKIE DOKE! I'M GOING OUTSIDE NOW! JUNIE B. JONES IS GOING OUTSIDE TO GET IN THE CAR!" I shouted louder.

Just then, Mother runned to get me.

"No, Junie B.! No! I'm not taking you to Lucille's, remember? Lucille's **nanna** is

picking you **up** at three o'clock. I told you that. I'm *sure* I did."

All of a sudden, my **shoulder**s got very **slump**ing. 'Cause I didn't actually remember that information, that's why.

"Darn it,[2]" I said very sad. "Three o'clock takes forever."

After that, I slumped to the table and ate my breakfast.

Then I sat on my front step.

And I **swing**ed on my swings.

And I read some books.

And I ate a cheese sandwich.

And I **count**ed to a million **bazillion**.

And I sat on my step some more.

---

2 **darn it** 'damn it(빌어먹을, 제기랄)'을 순화한 단어로, 못마땅하거나 짜증스러울 때 쓰는 속어적 표현.

And then guess what?

Three o'clock finally came!

I saw the big gold car in my **driveway**!

"HEY! SHE'S HERE! SHE'S HERE! SHE'S HERE!" I **yell**ed real **thrill**ed.

Mother and Daddy hurried to the door.

"Are you ready to go?" said Mother.

"READY!" I yelled. "JUNIE B. JONES IS READY TO GO!"

The richie nanna got out of her car.

I throwed my arms around her.

"HELLO, NANNA! HELLO! HELLO! I HAVE BEEN WAITING FOR YOU THE WHOLE **LIVELONG** DAY!"

Mother pulled me off of that woman.

"Sorry," she said. "I'm afraid Junie B. has a little **extra** energy in her. She's been

sitting on the step for hours."

I **leap**ed way high in the air.

"SITTING ON THE STEP!" I said. JUNIE B. JONES HAS BEEN SITTING ON THE STEP!"

Daddy and Mother carried my things to the big gold Cattle Act.

And guess what? When they opened the door, Lucille and that Grace were already in the **backseat**!

"LUCILLE! GRACE! I DIDN'T EVEN KNOW YOU WERE ALREADY HERE! AND SO THIS IS A **DELIGHTFUL** SURPRISE!"

I **reach**ed inside to try to **tickle** them. But Mother pulled my hand away.

"Please, Junie B. Don't start," she said.

I **salute**d her.

"Aye,[3] aye, Captain," I said real **hilarious**.

After that, I got in the car and I **bounce**d on the softie seat.

Only too bad for me. 'Cause I **accidental**ly bounced too high. And I **bang**ed my head on the **roof**.

The nanna did a **gasp**.

I **pat**ted her.

"Yeah, only that didn't even **faze** me," I said.

---

3 **aye** '네', '찬성'이라는 뜻으로 상대의 말에 동의할 때 사용하는 'yes'의 비격식적인 표현.

After that, I **buckle**d up my seat belt.

And I **wave**d good-bye to Mother and Daddy.

And the nanna drove us away.

5
Going to the Ball

Lucille was sitting in the middle.

She **whisper**ed real quiet to me and that Grace.

"**Beg** for my poodle," she said. "You *promised,* remember? You promised to beg for my poodle."

Me and that Grace looked and looked at each other. 'Cause we didn't actually want to do that **particular** thing.

Lucille **poke**d us.

"Come on! You *promised!*" she whispered. "You promised to beg!"

I did a **sigh**.

Then I thinked and thinked about what to say.

Finally, I took a deep breath.

"Hey, Nanna. Guess what? Lucille wants a poodle, **apparent**ly. And so could you buy her one, do you think?" I asked.

"Yes, could you?" asked that Grace. "'Cause she is making us beg you. Or else we can't spend the night."

The nanna's mouth came **all the way** open.

"Ohhhh. So *that's* what this is all about, huh? Well, my granddaughter knows perfectly well that I am **allergic** to dogs. So you can tell Lucille that a poodle is **out of the question**, I'm afraid."

I **pat**ted Lucille very **understanding**.

"A poodle is out of the question, we're afraid," I said.

Lucille kicked her feet up and down.

"Beg *harder*," she whispered. "You have to beg *harder*."

I did a **frown**.

"Are you **firm** on that, Nanna?" I asked.

"No poodle, Lucille!" said the nanna very **snappish**.

Lucille kicked her feet some more.

"I *knew* that **dumb** idea wouldn't work!" she **grouch**ed.

Just then, the car stopped in front of a

big **iron** gate.

Grace's eyes opened big and wide.

"Wow! This gate looks like a *castle* gate," she said.

Lucille smiled a **teeny** bit.

"It's not a castle gate, you **silly**head, Grace," she said. "This is the gate to my *house*."

The nanna pushed a button, and the gate opened right in front of our eyes.

"Hey, that button is like *magic!*" I said.

Lucille smiled bigger.

After that, the nanna drove down a long **driveway**. She stopped in front of a big, beautiful house.

Lucille jumped out of the car and ran inside.

Me and that Grace followed after her.

And guess what? Lucille's house was even beautifuller[1] on the *inside* than it was on the *outside!*

There was a beautiful long **row** of stairs. And a beautiful big **bowl** of flowers. And a beautiful, giant, **sparkly ceiling** light made out of glass.

I did a **gasp** at that **glisten**ing thing!

"That light **take**s **my breath**ing **away**!" I said.

Lucille **skip**ped all around in a circle.

She singed a loud song in our ears.

"SEE? SEE? I TOLD YOU I WAS RICH!

---

1 **beautifuller** 형용사 'beautiful'의 비교급을 잘못 만든 것으로, 올바른 표현은 'more beautiful'이다. 이 책에 나오는 'funner(more fun)'도 이와 같은 경우이다.

SEE? SEE? I TOLD YOU I WAS RICH!" she sang.

She **made** that song **up**, I believe.

After that, she took our hands and showed us all the rooms in her house.

She showed us the living room. And the dining room. And the kitchen. And the big giant patio.[2] And the daddy's office. And the mother's office. And the **family room**. And the pool[3] room where you play pool. And the outside pool where you swim. And the hot **tub.**[4] And the library.

---

2 **patio** 파티오 또는 중정. 건물에 둘러싸인 작은 외부 공간으로, 장식적인 타일을 바르거나 분수, 나무 등이 배치된다.

3 **pool** 포켓볼. 가늘고 긴 막대기로 공을 쳐서 테이블 모서리에 있는 구멍에 집어넣는 당구 경기의 하나. 여기에서 주니 B.는 포켓볼을 가리키는 'pool'과 수영장을 가리키는 'pool'을 이용해 말장난을 하고 있다.

4 **hot tub** 온수 욕조. 탕의 뜨거운 물과 압력을 이용해 마사지할 수 있는 대형 욕조.

And the **gym**. And the nanna's room. And the mother and daddy's room. And the **fancy** gold bathroom with the Jacuzzi.[5] And the brother's room. And a whole, whole **bunch** of guest rooms.

Then finally, Lucille showed us her very own bedroom!

And it looked like a bedroom where a princess lived!

Lucille's bed had a pink **frilly roof** on top of it.

"That is called a *canopy,*[6]" she explained. "It **match**es my pink silk[7] draperies[8] and

---

5 **jacuzzi** 자쿠지. 기포가 나오는 고급 마사지 욕조.

6 **canopy** 캐노피. 침대 위에 장식이나 방충 등을 목적으로 천장에 매달아서 늘어뜨리거나 고정하는 천.

7 **silk** 실크 또는 비단. 광택이 나며 재질이 매끄러운 고급 섬유.

8 **drapery** 드레이퍼리. 부드럽고 유연한 소재의 천을 사용하여 주름을 잡거나 자연스럽게 늘어뜨려서 장식용으로 사용하는 긴 커튼.

my pink silk **bedspread**. And my pink telephone. And my plush[9] pink **rug**. And my **wallpaper** with pink flowers in it.

"And see my TV? And my stereo?[10] And my computer? And my CD player?"

She pointed to the corner. "And did you **notice** all of my big **stuff**ed animals standing over there?" she asked.

My eyes **pop**ped out at those giant guys. The **giraffe** was bigger than me even!

Me and that Grace ran to play with them.

"NO! STOP! DON'T!" shouted Lucille. "YOU'RE NOT ALLOWED TO TOUCH

---

9 **plush** 플러시. 벨벳과 비슷하나 길고 보드라운 보풀이 있는 천으로 주로 아동복, 인형, 가구 등에 사용된다.

10 **stereo** 스테레오. 두 개 이상의 스피커로 서로 다른 소리를 재생하여 입체적인 음향을 느끼게 하는 재생 장치.

THEM! THEY ARE JUST FOR SHOW!"

"Huh?" said that Grace.

"What?" I said. "How come?"

"Because they were expensive, *that's* how come," she said. "Those animals costed my nanna a **fortune**."

"Oh," I said kind of **disappoint**ed.

"Oh," said that Grace.

We sat down on Lucille's bed.

Lucille shouted at us again. "NO! GET UP! YOU'RE NOT ALLOWED TO SIT THERE! THAT BEDSPREAD IS JUST FOR SHOW!"

Me and that Grace springed right off of there.

Lucille quick **smooth**ed the **material** with her hand.

"Don't you two know *anything?*" she said. "This bedspread is made out of *silk,* I told you. I'm not allowed to get it **soil**ed."

"Oh," I said.

"Oh," said that Grace.

After that, Lucille skipped over to her **dresser**. And she **press**ed a button on her mirror.

A **million** bazillion lights came on!

"Look at this," she said. "This is my very own **professional makeup** mirror! It is the same kind of mirror that they use for movie stars. My nanna brought it all the way from Hollywood,[11] California!"

Me and that Grace runned to the sparkly

---

11 **Hollywood** 할리우드. 미국 캘리포니아주(州) 로스앤젤레스 서북쪽에 있는 지역으로, 세계적인 영화 산업의 중심지이다.

mirror. We looked at ourselves in the bright lights.

Then we **stick**ed out our **tongue**s and made funny faces.

Lucille quick turned it off.

"It is *not* a toy!" she grouched.

After that, me and that Grace just stood

very **still**. And we didn't touch anything.

"This is going to be a long evening," I said kind of quiet.

Only just then, something very wonderful happened!

Lucille's nanna came in the room! And she was carrying a big box of **dress-up** clothes!

"I thought you little gals[12] might have fun with some of my old evening **gowns**," she said real nice. "They're **as old as the hills**. But they're still quite **stunning**."

Lucille runned to the box **speedy** quick.

"Let's play Cinderella![13]" she said.

---

12 **gal** '여자아이'를 뜻하는 비격식적인 호칭.

13 **Cinderella** 신데렐라. 새어머니와 두 명의 새언니에게 구박을 받던 주인공 신데렐라가 요정의 도움으로 궁중 무도회에 참석했다가 잃어버린 유리 구두 한 짝이 인연이 되어 왕자와 결혼하는 이야기.

She pulled out a beautiful, sparkly pink gown.

"I'M CINDERELLA!" she shouted.

Then that Grace **shove**d me out of her way. And she runned to the box, too.

She pulled out a sparkly *blue* gown.

"I'M THE **FAIRY** GODMOTHER![14]" she **yell**ed.

I did a **huffy** breath at those two. 'Cause now I had to be the ugly **stepsister**s, probably.

I **bend**ed down and **search**ed through the box very **careful**.

Then **all of a sudden**, my hands felt

---

14 **fairy godmother** 요정 대모. 동화 신데렐라에 등장하는 요정으로 파티에 가지 못해 낙심한 신데렐라에게 호박 마차와 유리 구두를 만들어 주며 공주로 변신시킨다.

something long and **silky** and softie.

I quick pulled it out of there.

The nanna's whole face **light**ed up.

"Oh my **goodness**! My old **feather boa**![15]" she said. "Why,[16] I haven't seen that thing in years!"

I danced all around with that lovely thing.

"I love this, Nanna! I love this old feather boa!"

Just then, another great idea popped in my brain.

"Hey! I know! I will be the famous singer that sings at Cinderella's ball!"

---

15 feather boa 깃털 목도리. 모피나 깃털 등으로 만든 길고 둥근 여성용 목도리.

16 why 여기에서는 '왜'라는 뜻의 의문사가 아니라 '아니!', '어머!'라는 의미의 감탄사로 쓰였다.

Lucille and Grace looked funny at me.

"What singer?" said Lucille.

"There's no singer," said that Grace.

I **stamp**ed my foot at them.

"Yes, there is! There is, too, a singer! And I am her! And my name is Florence the Famous Singer! And I will be performing

show **tune**s from the **hit** musical[17] *Annie!*[18] So there!"

Lucille and Grace **shrug**ged their

17 **musical** 뮤지컬. 미국에서 발달한 현대 음악극의 한 형태로 음악, 노래, 무용을 결합하여 큰 무대에서 상연하는 종합 무대 예술이다.

18 **Annie** 만화 '고아 소녀 애니(Little Orphan Annie)'를 원작으로 한 뮤지컬. 고아원에 남겨진 주인공 애니(Annie)가 그녀의 순수함을 알아본 워벅스(Warbucks) 씨를 만나 그의 딸로 입양되기까지 벌어지는 이야기를 다룬다.

shoulders at me.

Then they **dressed up** in their beautiful gowns.

And they went to the ball.

And I sang "The Sun Will Come Out Tomorrow.[19]"

---

19 **The Sun Will Come Out Tomorrow** 뮤지컬 '애니(Annie)'의 대표곡 'Tomorrow'의 가사. 힘든 일이 있어도 희망찬 내일이 올 것이라고 노래하는 주인공 애니의 밝고 명랑한 성격을 표현한 곡이다.

6
Bouncing

After we finished playing Cinderella, the **nanna** called us to dinner.

Me and Lucille and that Grace **skip**ped into the big dining room. We sat at a long, **shiny** table.

Pretty soon, Lucille's nanna came in from the kitchen. And she gave us our dinner.

And guess what?

Its name was beans and Frank![1]

"**Hurray**!" I said. "Hurray for beans and Frank! 'Cause this is my favorite kind of home cooking!"

The nanna did a teeny smile.

"Well, we usually have a cook. But I gave her the night off," she said.

After that, the nanna **pour**ed milk into beautiful **sparkly** glasses.

"Oooo, Nanna! These are your best **crystal** glasses!" said Lucille real **thrill**ed. "I love these expensive things!"

"Me, too! I love these expensive things, too!" I said.

Only too bad for me. 'Cause nobody

---

1 **beans and Frank** 강낭콩과 소시지를 토마토 소스에 함께 졸여 만드는 스튜의 한 종류.

even told me that crystal glasses were very heavy.

And so when I picked up my glass, it **slip**ped right out of my hand.

And it fell on the floor!

And it broke into lots of pieces!

Lucille's whole mouth came open.

"OH NO! YOU BROKE IT! YOU BROKE MY NANNA'S CRYSTAL GLASS!"

The nanna's face was **reddish** and **scrunch**y.

"Sorry, Nanna," I said real soft. "Sorry I broke your crystal glass."

The nanna **suck**ed her **cheek**s way into her head.

"Let's just try to be more **careful**, shall we, dear?" she said.

I **bob**bed my head up and down.

"We shall," I said back.

After that, I ate my beans and Frank very careful. Only pretty soon, my Frank **spill**ed off my fork. And he **land**ed on the nanna's white **tablecloth**.

"OH NO!" **holler**ed Lucille. "THAT'S MY NANNA'S GOOD LINEN[2] TABLECLOTH! SHE BROUGHT IT **ALL THE WAY** FROM IRELAND!"

The nanna's face was **twist**y and **puffy**.

I quick pushed my plate away from me.

My **stomach** felt in a tight **knot**.

"Yeah, only guess what? I am not actually hungry anymore. And so I will

---

2 **linen** 리넨. 아마(亞麻)라는 식물에서 뽑은 실로 짠 얇은 천. 주로 셔츠, 손수건, 실내 장식품 등을 만드는 데 쓰인다.

just sit here and not spill anything, I think."

The nanna cleaned up my **mess**es with a wet cloth.

After she finished, she brought us chocolate ice cream for **dessert**.

Only too bad for me. 'Cause a teeny **plop** of ice cream dropped right off my spoon. And it landed on my chair cushion.

The nanna did a big breath.

"You're a bit of a **bull** in a **china** shop,[3] aren't you, dear?" she said.

"Sorry, Nanna," I said. "Sorry, sorry, sorry."

The nanna **pat**ted my hand very **stiff**ish.[4]

---

3 **a bull in a china shop** 직역하면 '도자기 가게 안의 황소'라는 뜻으로, '주의가 요구되는 상황에서 거칠게 구는 사람'이라는 뜻의 숙어이다.

4 **stiffish** 주니 B.가 만들어 낸 말로 단어 'stiff(뻣뻣한)' 뒤에 '-ish'를 붙여 '뻣뻣하게'라는 의미의 부사로 사용하였다.

"Quite all right," she said kind of **mumbly**.

After that, I got down from the table. And me and my friends went back to Lucille's room.

And guess what?

Things got funner!

'Cause Lucille said we could play with the games in her **closet**! **On account of** they weren't even expensive!

First, we played **Chute**s and Ladders.[5] Then we played Twister[6] and Bingo[7] and

5 **Chutes and Ladders** 슈츠 앤 래더즈. 주사위를 굴려 나온 수만큼 전진하면서, 미끄럼틀을 만나면 따라 내려가고 사다리를 만나면 타고 올라가는 보드게임. 마지막 칸에 먼저 도달하면 승리한다.

6 **Twister** 트위스터. 여러 가지 색깔이 칠해진 판 위에 서서 회전판의 바늘이 가리키는 색깔에 두 손과 두 발을 올려 놓는 게임.

7 **Bingo** 빙고. 정방형의 표에 숫자를 여러 종류로 배열해 적고, 사회자가 임의로 부르는 숫자를 가장 빠르게 가로, 세로, 또는 사선으로 연결하는 것을 겨루는 게임.

Chinese checkers[8] and Tic-Tac-Toad[9] and Candyland.[10] Plus also we played Let's **Spin** Till We Get Real **Dizzy** and Fall Down.

And guess what? I didn't even break anything!

"Hey! I think I am **get**ting **the hang of** this party!" I said very happy.

Just then, the nanna **knock**ed on Lucille's door.

"Time for you ladies to put your

---

8 **Chinese checkers** 차이니즈 체커 또는 다이아몬드 게임. 다이아몬드 모양의 말판 위에서 자기 앞에 놓인 말을 건너편으로 먼저 모두 이동한 사람이 이기는 보드게임.

9 **Tic-Tac-Toad** 틱택토드. 두 명이 번갈아 가며 3×3 판에 O와 X를 그려 그것이 가로, 세로, 혹은 대각선상에 위치하면 이기는 보드게임인 '틱택토(Tic-Tac-Toe)'에 '두꺼비(toad)' 일러스트를 그려 넣은 보드게임.

10 **Candyland** 캔디랜드. 카드를 뒤집어 나온 색깔과 동일한 색깔의 다음 칸으로 게임판 위의 말을 이동시키면서 캔디성에 먼저 도착해 왕을 찾으면 승리하는 보드게임.

pajamas on," she told us.

I danced all around the room real happy.

"Hurray!" I said "Hurray for pajamas! 'Cause I brought my favorites!"

I quick put them on.

"See them, Nanna? See how **biggish** and **baggish**[11] they are? That is how come they feel so comfortable!"

The nanna's eyes looked down at me.

"How very . . . ***charming***," she said.

Just then, that Grace jumped right in front of me.

"Look at mine, Nanna!" she said. "See mine? My pajamas have neon-green[12]

---

11 baggish 주니 B.가 만들어 낸 말로 단어 'baggy(헐렁한)' 뒤에 '-ish'를 붙여 '헐렁한 것 같은', '헐렁한 듯한'이라는 의미의 형용사로 사용하였다.

12 neon 네온 (컬러). 채도와 명도가 높은 색상을 통틀어 이르는 말.

polka dotties on them!"

"How very . . . ***colorful,***" said the nanna.

All of a sudden, Lucille popped out of her big closet.

"Ta-da![13] Look at *me,* everyone! I am wearing my **beauteous** pink satin[14] **nightie**! See me? See how lovely I look! I look like a **gorgeous** model in this thing!" she said.

Lucille let me and that Grace feel her **material**.

"How very . . . ***smoothie,***" I said.

After that, me and Grace un**roll**ed our

---

13 **ta-da** '기대하시라', '짠'이라는 의미로 주로 사람이나 물건을 처음 보일 때 내는 소리.

14 **satin** 새틴. 광택이 있고 매끄러운 천으로, 주로 장식적인 여성복, 핸드백, 모자 등에 사용된다.

sleeping bags on the floor. And the nanna took the silk **bedspread** off Lucille's bed.

"Time to get your **beauty sleep**, Princess," she told Lucille.

Then those two kissed and **hug**ged good night. And the nanna shut the door.

Only guess what?

Lucille didn't even get in bed. She kept **twirl**ing all around in her pink satin night**gown**.

"This is how models twirl," she said. "They twirl so you can see their fronts and their backs."

Lucille wouldn't stop twirling.

"See my front? See my back?" she said.

Me and that Grace got up on her bed to watch her twirl.

Lucille's bed was soft and **cushy**.

We bounced up there a teeny bit.

Lucille stopped twirling.

"Hey! Don't!" she said. "That bed is for

beauty sleep *only!*"

I patted her bed very **admiring**.

"Yeah, only it's too bad we can't actually play up here. 'Cause this mattress[15] is a ***bouncy*** one," I said.

Just then, Lucille's face did a **sneaky** smile.

"Want to bounce?" she said real soft. "Want to really, *really* bounce?"

She **tip**py-**toe**d to her door and looked down the **hall**.

"Come on," she whispered. "Follow me."

I **grab**bed Philip Johnny Bob and followed after Lucille and that Grace.

---

15 mattress 매트리스. 속에 스프링이나 스펀지 등을 넣어 푹신하게 만든 침대용 깔개 또는 두툼한 침구.

We tippy-toed down the hall and around the corner.

Then Lucille opened the door to a big guest room. And there was a **giant** bed in that place!

"See it!" she said. "See how ***huge*** that bed is? My nanna had it specially made **in case** we have tall **company**!"

Lucille quick shut the door after us.

"Come on! Let's go!" she said.

And so all of us runned to the big bed speedy quick! And we jumped and jumped and jumped on that thing!

I sang a **joyful** song.

It is called "Jumping, Jumping, Jumping on the Giant Bed."

"JUMPING . . . JUMPING . . . JUMPING

ON THE GIANT BED," I sang.

Only too bad for me. 'Cause all of a sudden, I remembered something very important. And it is called *Mother and Daddy said no jumping.*

I got off the bed speedy fast.

"Yeah, only here's the problem," I said. "I am not actually allowed to jump. 'Cause Mother and Daddy said *no jumping.* And so you guys should stop jumping, too. 'Cause that would be **polite** of you."

Lucille and that Grace didn't pay **attention** to me.

That is how come I had to get back on the giant bed and shout in their faces.

"STOP JUMPING, I SAID! 'CAUSE I AM NOT ALLOWED TO JUMP! AND YOU

GUYS SHOULDN'T JUMP, TOO!"

Grace **spring**ed way high in the air.

"Who's jumping? I'm not jumping," she said.

She **giggle**d very **silly**. "I'm *bouncing!*"

Just then, my whole face got happy.

I hugged and hugged that girl.

'Cause Mother and Daddy didn't say I couldn't *bounce!*

After that, I bounced and bounced and bounced.

"BOUNCING . . . BOUNCING . . . BOUNCING ON THE GIANT BED," I sang.

I bounced till **sweat** came on my head.

Then I **flop**ped down on the bed to **rest**.

I flopped on a **plumpery**[16] **pillow**.

"Oooo, Lucille! This is the most plumpery pillow I ever even saw!" I told her.

"Of *course* it is, silly," said Lucille. "That's because my nanna has all her pillows handmade in Sweden."

I quick **swing**ed the plumpery pillow over to my friend Grace.

"Grace! Hey, Grace! Feel how plumpery this pillow is!" I said.

Only Grace didn't actually see it coming. And it **accidental**ly hit her in the head.

I **peek**ed at her under that thing.

---

16 plumpery 주니 B.가 만들어 낸 말로 단어 'plump(통통한)'를 강조하여 말한 표현.

"Yeah, only that did not even **harm** you, I **bet**. 'Cause plumpery pillows don't hurt people. Right, Grace. Right?"

That Grace did a teeny **grin**.

Then she took the plumpery pillow off her head. And she swinged it all around. And she hit me in the **tummy**!

"Ooomph!" I said.

Then I laughed and laughed.

"Hey! I was right! Plumpery pillows *don't* hurt people!"

After that, I hit Lucille in the head with my plumpery pillow. Plus also, I hit Grace again.

Then those guys got their own plumpery pillows. And all of us kept on hitting each other very fun!

Only just then, a mistake happened. 'Cause I didn't even know there was a **rip** in my plumpery pillow. And so the next time I hit Grace, all of my **feather**s

exploded out of it!

There was a million **bazillion** of those **floaty** things.

They filled the whole air, **practical**ly.

Lucille did a **gasp**.

That Grace did a gasp, too.

I danced around very giggling.

"HEY! IT'S SNOWING!" I said. "IT'S SNOWING! IT'S SNO—"

Just then, the door swinged opened very fast!

It was Lucille's nanna!

She saw me holding the broken plumpery pillow!

My heart **pound**ed hard inside of me.

"Hello," I said very nervous. "How are you today? I am fine. **Except** I am having a little bit of a feather problem, **apparent**ly."

The nanna walked at me very slow.

Then she took my pillow out of my hands.

And she hided her face in that **flat**ty thing.

And she didn't come out for a real long time.

7
Peeping

After a while, the nanna took us back to Lucille's room.

Me and Philip Johnny Bob got in our **sleeping bag speedy** fast.

Then that Grace got in her sleeping bag, too. And Lucille got into her softie bed.

"Not one more peep out of you girls," said the nanna very **grouchy**. "Do you hear me? Not one more *peep*."

She turned off the light and shut the door.

I stayed quiet a real long time. 'Cause I was **scare**d of that woman, that's why.

All of a sudden, I heard a **teeny** voice.

"Peep!" it said. "Peep, peep, peep!"

It was Lucille.

Me and that Grace **giggle**d out loud at her.

"Peep," said that Grace.

"Peep," I said.

Peep, said Philip Johnny Bob.

Then pretty soon, all of us were peeping all over the place.

"Peep, peep, peep, *peep*. Peep, peep, peep, *peep*."

Lucille kept on peeping louder and

louder and louder.

"PEEP! PEEP! PEEP!" she said.

Also, she was giggling very hard.

Finally, me and that Grace sat up in our sleeping bags. We **stare**d at that girl.

"Lucille is peeping out of **control**," said that Grace.

"Maybe she is overly tired," I said. "Overly tired makes your brain go **silly**."

"PEEP!" said Lucille. "PEEP! PEEP! PEEP! PEEP! PEEP!"

Just then, Lucille's nanna opened the door again.

"**SILENCE**!" she **yell**ed real **scary**.

Shivers came on my **skin**.

Then all of us quick **crawl**ed under our **cover**s again.

And we closed our eyes.

And we didn't say another peep.

8
Morning

Morning came very early.

It was still dark outside.

I **jiggle**d Lucille and that Grace.

"I'm hungry," I said. "Are you guys hungry. I am really, *really* hungry."

I shook them some more.

"Let's eat. You wanna eat? I really, *really* wanna eat."

Finally, Lucille and that Grace **yawn**ed

and **stretch**ed.

Then all of us put on our bath**robe**s and our **slipper**s. And we went down the **hall** to get the **nanna** for breakfast.

Lucille shaked her real gentle.

"Wake up, Nanna," she **whisper**ed.

"Wake up, Nanna," said that Grace.

"Wake up, Nanna," I said.

The nanna did a **snore**.

That's how come we had to pull her up by her arms. And we turned a bright light in her face.

The nanna yawned real big.

It was not **pleasant**.

After that, she got her robe and slippers. And she went **downstairs** with us.

We sat at the long dining room table

again.

The nanna passed out cereal **bowl**s.

"Oh, Nanna! These are the **brand-new china** bowls you bought in France! These are my favorites!" said Lucille.

All of a sudden, I felt a **knot** in my

stomach again.

I **tap**ped on the nanna's hand.

"Yeah, only here's the problem. I think I would like to have a plastic cereal bowl. 'Cause plastic is more my style."

The nanna **roll**ed **her eyes** way up at the

ceiling. I looked up there, too. But I didn't see anything.

"I don't *own* any plastic cereal bowls," she said.

After that, she brought in the orange juice. And she **pour**ed it into **teeny crystal** glasses.

I got down from my chair.

"Yeah, only guess what? I think I will just stand here and not eat. Or else I might **spill** something again," I said.

The nanna looked and looked at me.

Then she went into the kitchen and she brought me back a banana.

"Here. Try this," she said kind of nicer.

I did a smile.

Then I ate my banana very **careful**.

And I didn't spill a drop.

Mother **pick**ed me **up** at nine o'clock.

She came into the nanna's big, beautiful house to get me.

"My! What a lovely home you have here," she said to the nanna.

Then Mother walked to the big bowl of beautiful flowers. And she tried to smell those lovely things.

"NO! DON'T! THEY ARE JUST FOR SHOW PROBABLY!" I **holler**ed.

After that, I said good-bye to my friends. And I thanked the nanna. And I quick pulled Mother out of that house. Or else she might break something, that's why.

I runned down the steps and got in

my car. Then I **rub**bed my hand on the **backseat**.

It was not as soft as the nanna's backseat.

I smiled very **relieve**d.

"It's good to be back," I said.

Mother drove down the long **driveway**.

My stomach **growl**ed real loud.

"Guess what? My **tummy** is still hungry for breakfast. 'Cause I didn't actually eat much this morning," I said.

Mother laughed.

"I **swear**, Junie B. Your stomach is a **bottomless pit**,[1]" she said.

Just then, another great idea **pop**ped

---

1 **bottomless pit** 많이 먹는 사람을 이르는 말.

into my head!

"Mother! Hey, Mother! Maybe you and me can stop at Grandma Miller's for breakfast! 'Cause she fixes blueberry pancakes every Sunday morning! And blueberry pancakes is my favorite breakfast in the whole **entire** world!"

Mother thinked about my offer.

Then all of a sudden, she turned around the car. And we drove to my grandma Miller's house. And we were just in time for blueberry pancakes!

We ate a **million bazillion** of those delicious things!

Plus also I drank orange juice out of a plastic glass!

"**Hurray**!" I said. "Hurray for plastic!"

Then me and Grandma Miller **hug**ged and hugged.

And guess what else?

I think I like my **regular** nanna just perfect.